Letters to a first love
from the future

Andy Armitage

Published by Half Moon Books 2018
an imprint of OWF Press Community Interest Company
Otley Courthouse, Courthouse Street, Otley, LS21 3AN

Reprinted 2018

www.halfmoonbooks.co.uk

ISBN 978-0-9957642-1-7

Half Moon cover design: Nick Palmer.

Printed & bound by ImprintDigital.com, UK.

Acknowledgements

'The playing fields' won First Prize in the Leeds Museum Poetry Competition
2017; 'Et in Arcadia ego' was Highly Commended in the YorkMix / York
Literature Festival Poetry Competition 2018. The poems 'Moonstruck' and
'Among School Children' first appeared in *Dream Catcher* and an early
fragment of 'Hoarder' first appeared in *Strix*.

Thanks to Nick Lonsdale, Clare Proctor, the 'Hulman Beings' (Ian Harker,
Andrew Lambeth, Anna Sutcliffe, Tom Kelly, Rose Journeaux), Helen Mort,
Tom Weir, Amina Alyal, Alicia Fernandez, Emma Storr, John Foggin, Joe
Williams, Mark Connors, Bec Edwards, the Leeds Writers Circle, my friends
from Arvon, the Hurst, 2017 and my friends on the Kim Moore poetry
residential course in St Ives, April 2018 for looking at drafts of the poems
and offering encouragement and criticism. Thanks to Col Griffiths for his
photographic work and promotional design work and to Mizue Bates for her
ongoing support and encouragement.

Contents

Snapshot

Who took that photograph of us
in the empty playground
after the bell had gone
as we loitered between long
mechanical French kisses?
Somebody rescued that moment
from the dark room of oblivion.
I might have forgotten
the sweep of brown hair
you'd tilt from your eye.
I might have forgotten the glow
of your untouched skin
but someone fixed us there,
our heads leant together
in idiot hope
with all our history ahead of us,
your blouse buttoned at the collar,
my chaste hands at my sides
like the hands on a stopped clock.

Sally

On the last day I didn't love you
I was fifteen, and the universe
was the size of a village.
That summer me and my mates
kicked about the streets,
haunted bus shelters and ginnels,
wandered into that Friday night
looking for a secluded spot to drink.

On the graveyard path between
the off-licence and church
a group of girls passed on their way
to the fair, and you –
dark haired with a gypsy tan,
in ripped 501s and Docs.
It was as though I'd stepped into the road
looking in the wrong direction
and heard a screech of brakes behind me.

In the candyfloss air
between the waltzers and dodgems,
amid a confusion of coloured lightbulbs,
above the laughter and shrieks,
I heard your friends calling you
and hurried home hiding my dread
and excitement, as though
I'd left the shop without paying
for the name pressed here
among these pages,
like a flower.

Moonstruck

Each night I lay in the dark hours
that circled your light
and tried to blink away
our encounters.

My mind had caught hold the string
of your rising moon,
buoyed me to such heights,
letting go was suddenly unthinkable.

And so, drunk with sleeplessness,
I hung about the stars
admiring your wonderful
alignments,

rehearsed how I'd tell you
that while you slept five miles away,
I heard you breathing in the wind;
how each car that passed carried

a sigh over the wet streets between us;
how your moon lit my brief dreams
so that every word you never spoke
rang in my ears when I awoke.

Among school children

When the bell went
there was a scrape of chairs
and we'd shoulder our way
into that bristling forest of green voices
not long above ground,
all reached towards the light.

I searched for breadcrumb rumours
of your whereabouts.
I just wanted to pass by,
to catch your eye,
though the gift of a glance
tangled my feet and tongue.

I made myself famous among classrooms
with stunts of disobedience.
I wanted my name in your ear,
to learn some lesson about daring.

Under a practised nonchalance
I hid the hurt of my hope
for a year of hours
until that time I found you alone
on the stairs and pulled you aside
and asked you.

The snare

I snared you with laughter,
offered up private humiliations,
public displays,
to the broad crescent of your mouth.

I discovered a talent for the absurd,
reeling you in with my clownish
performances. When you laughed
your eyes narrowed

and the flash of your pupils
was like a flash of skirt,
catching my breath,
holding me fast.

Conspiracy

I walked along the railway lines
all night, all night,
over dull percussive stones,
just to throw mud at your window.

You whispered me in
and I remember your delight
that a boy would walk all night
to steal a kiss from your mouth
in the hour of thieves.

Where did your eyes find their light
as we sat in the inky dark
your body still warm from your bed
in my cool hands?

We held our breath,
hearing a lightswitch
and the approach of footsteps.
As the door handle turned
you closed your eyes
and let your head fall
on my shoulder.
Without an alibi –
I closed mine.

But it was your mother
who hissed your name
and it was you
and not your father
who showed me to the door.

I walked along the railway lines
all night, all night,
the stones singing under my shoes
a stolen kiss on my mouth.

Et in Arcadia ego

We are in the dark
on the swings in the Rec,
a plastic bag of cans at our feet.

You're sitting astride me
in those ripped jeans and Docs,
telling me who you are.

The voices of our friends are cast about us,
each shadow finding its edges
under that big wheel of constellations.

Here the moon is always waxing.
We know nothing of years or distance.
Your eyes are brimming with dead stars.

Do not let go my hand just yet.

Cross Gates Station

Last minute, the lines would be hissing
with the last train's approach
as I tumbled onto the platform
like a glowing coal dropped beneath

the hearth to cool in the evening air.
Breathless and giddy with frustration
I'd adjust to the sudden drop in pressure
like a diver ascended too quickly,

dazed and euphoric, disentangling
your phantom limbs, the pressure of your
budding breasts, my mouth bruised
with your mouth, the taste of you on my fingers.

Cross Gates station – station of my cross.
The holy place where I'd alight
each school night, thrilled and thwarted,
to return and return from my destination.

The playing fields

Do you remember the playing fields
where we lay that bright April morning
when everything was green and awakening?
Our skinny bodies couched in the grass
under that solitary oak, and the silence

filled with your voice, strange to me
as the chatter of a blackbird. I held you
tight as a bud holds its flower
and tried to staunch the wound of myself
as you unfurled in my hands.

Did you ever go back to the playing fields?
The grass still offers its uneven mattress
and the plump trees that hide the graveyard
have not grown crooked with age but reach out
hesitantly in the uncertain breeze that lifted

a strand of your hair. There are broken wings
and little skulls under the thickening hedgerows
but to me it is as though nothing has ever wintered.
And the church bell that rang out the hours
of that first morning still echoes down the years.

Sunday morning

We are lying in the bed of my first bedsit
in the wake of another big Saturday night
because we are young.

You are waitressing at lunch
so soon the mattress will lurch and rise
and I'll turn to see you step
into your knickers
and sit at the dresser
to tie back your hair,
apply mascara to your lashes.

Glancing past your reflection
You'll see me watching
and smile, then purse your lips
to redden them.

When you reach for your blouse
I will tell you to 'come back to bed'
because we still have time
and maybe you'll believe me.

Maybe you'll check your watch
and grab your keys
and kiss me
and tell me 'later'

and I will believe you
because we are young
and have forever.

A room with a double bed

I found us a place to plant
our roots, a place to bed
under a dim bulb.

But you could not bloom
in the stony ground of my petty
ambitions. I held you too tight

as though a stinging nettle –
afraid to loosen my grip.
I pruned and bullied

all that reached beyond us,
thinking you thrived
as you climbed the walls

starved of oxygen and light,
reached through the curtains
and crept out the window,

a shred of green burning in my hands.

The wound

I was less your lover than your disciple
following my heart's unruly compass
while you led the way to paradise.

If I'd believed, we might have been alright
but some demon you'd not exorcised
whispered in my ear

how the world turned when you went by,
that you were a false prophet
and I was a fool.

I sat in the dark listening to the voice
as I waited for you to return
from a night out with your friends,

your sweater draped over a chair
remembering something of the shape
that appeared in the doorway

to hear what the voice had to say.
I remember how your shoulders trembled
as I counted your tears.

I just couldn't believe you'd come back
until I'd touched the wound under your ribs.

Giving up

You burned in my hands
like a cigarette.
What could I do
but lift you to my lips?

And what alchemy
in those vague blue kisses
that simplified my appetites?
First thing in the morning

last thing at night
my heart raced
as you set alight
to mix our bloods.

You're no more to blame
for that intake of breath
than the flame that brings
the moth against the window pane.

Nottingham Trent

When you told me you were going
to university I couldn't believe
you'd risk everything for a certificate.

On my weekend visits I tried
to get us back on track but faltered
at each corner as you indicated

a left or right, halting me at particular
crossings. One morning I nipped out
for milk and struggled to find my way

back to your bed as this strange new city
withheld its knowledge of you.
I waited in your car and watched you

disappear into the university campus
to hand in an assignment, trailed you
around the aisles of a supermarket,

losing you and finding you again as you
carelessly dropped groceries into a trolley.
Following you home with the bags

I sensed another walking alongside us.
When I turned to look, you vanished
around the corner ahead of us.

Dear John

It's a messy business
asking the heart to stop.
There's a metal room

where that struggle with forever
happens. It stinks of blood
and shit. There's that awful noise

the knife hacks at in the trachea,
as the carotid artery sprays its jet
over the vinyl apron and slippery floor,

there's that look in the swivelled
eyeball as the heart clenches
a defiant fist. It's best to not look,

best to plug your ears
and think of that room as a letterbox
through which endings are posted

to land on the mat softly.

Lullaby

O love, as you lay asleep in my arms
I can feel the tides of your breathing,
the pulse in your hot body,
smell the scent of your hair –
so that I whisper 'I love you'
to your dark lashes.
But you cannot hear me. You are somewhere else.
You can no more hear me
than hear the words I write tonight,
so many years away in your future
where you have another lover,
another city, another name.
If you could hear me I would tell you
I do not envy your children.
Though your eyes follow them to their beds
I do not envy them.
Though they wear the smell of your hair
I do not envy them.
Though they live in the house of your laughter
I do not envy them.
Though they bear the weight of your kisses
I do not envy your children.
For many years from where I write
they have yet to learn to live
in a world in which you can't be found.

Midas

Everything you touched
became precious

so I lay on the shape
you left in the sheets

and bloodied my mouth
on a broken glass

stamped with your lips
for a last sip of wine.

Hoarder

It's difficult knowing where to start,
clearing a space to live in
among the clutter of the heart,
curating a beginning.

There's a shame in letting go,
in saying a thing cannot be mended,
but the relics of my other lives
disturb my sleep, they prevent

me from sitting down to eat.
I root among bags and boxes
for something mislaid
in a jumble of attachments.

It's getting so I cannot turn around
or close a door behind me.

A longitude of longing

I have crossed the Date Line
into yesterday
to reach the country of my youth.

A beggar from the badlands
with post-dated papers,
a happy cartographer

to map each feature of your face,
to trace a finger over the hills
of your breasts, their sweet rosettes.

I'll take the old paths
over the plateau of your belly,
to visit your valleys

and tease a song
from your lips
in the old tongue,

to search the still lake
of your eyes
for a future that never happened.

17th October

It's just a space on the calendar
kept respectfully blank,
like the tag on an unsent gift.

A date upon which things happen
somewhere else. Like the night
your father bundled your mother

and the overnight-bag into the van
because you wanted to be born.
And the light from his headlamps split

my curtains and rolled over the bedroom ceiling
so that I opened my eyes
and began to cry until my mother

lifted me from the cot
and told me to not be afraid
because it had only been a dream.

Each year I tell myself – it was only a dream
while someone else unwraps your gifts
and you lay there, naked as a baby.

Eurydice

You've been gone a long time
and have forgotten so much
even your own face
is only half-remembered
in the worldly grin
you wear among these bones
and leathery ribbons.
Is this the pelvis I nestled in?
But I knew you here in the dark
from that dim spark when
our shadows met.
I have come to learn how long
you have been without song
and if a song can move you yet,
of how I first heard your name
above the din of the fair
or how on the playing fields
the wind lifted a strand of your hair.
Each thinks his own is beautiful
but you were loveliest of all
so let these songs stand in for what I lack
because I could not but look back.

Eucharist

You're too young to know about endings
and I'm too old to believe in them.

But know this – I have been faithful
as a widower in my old religion,

keeping your candle alight.
Your eyes look back at me

from the faces of other women,
the dark priestesses

that lift a glass of wine
to my mouth

with your hand,
that put your arms around me

as I lift them,
light as loaves

and lay them on your altar
to eat again of your body.